FROM ONE YOUNG SOUL TO ANOTHER: LESSONS FROM THE MANY CHALLENGES OF EARLY ADULTHOOD

CONTENTS

Foreword
Chapter 1: Losing Yourself in Somebody Else
Chapter 2: The Never-Ending Self-Improvement Game
Chapter 3: Finding a Job Is Tougher Than It Seems
Chapter 4: Getting More From Less Through Minimalism
Chapter 5: The Pressure to Stay Busy
Chapter 6: Overthinking is Personal Enslavement
Chapter 7: Comparison Will Cause Suffering
Chapter 8: Finding Our Identity
Chapter 9: Giving Up the Need for Control
Conclusion

FOREWORD

Days like today are tough.

I value my Sundays. Well, for 21 weeks a year. Sunday is the one day a week where no matter what else is going on in my life, I clear my schedule to sit on my ass and watch football all day.

During this day of wonderful laziness, I put myself through the pain of playing fantasy football.

Today, I played fantasy football very badly. This brings down my mood significantly. In some cases, losing in fantasy football has no stakes: it's just a loss on my record and nothing more. Those losses don't bother me much.

In other cases, I have money on the line. And *those* losses lead me down a rabbit hole of "what if?" "Why the hell did I play him?" "I was so close to playing that guy and he did way better than my guy!" "I feel terrible that he got hurt, but I feel just as bad for myself that I played him in fantasy."

If you're not a sports fan, you may not know. But, yes: we can be terrible people. Or at least very selfish and self-centered.

Days like this are tough because I'm trying to re-shift my priorities. I wish it was as simple as a finger-snap to alter how certain things make me feel and my reactions to them, but it's just not that easy.

For weeks now, my struggles in fantasy football have upset me on Sunday—the day that is supposed to be full of detoxing and relaxation. My day of easy-going joy turns into pain and self-loathing because of fantasy football.

So, I finally did it: I withdrew all the money from my accounts and deleted the apps. I will no longer be tempted to fill my Sundays with fruitless and inevitable anger.

Believe it or not, this was a big step for me—and an example of how I'm changing my life, one small decision at a time.

This year has been full of these small little changes. By the end of it, 2020 will probably go down as the most productive year of my life. Yes, I know—2020 sucked for everyone. How could I have found anything positive to take away?

It wasn't a great year for me, either, but it's in those years where the greatest lessons come. Adversity challenges us and makes us stronger. 2020 was the year of adversity, and I'm proud to say that I will come out better.

Back in February, I looked forward to a productive year for myself, but in a much different way than reality had in mind. I was going to cover the Big Ten Men's Basketball Tournament and add a great experience to my resume. I was going to graduate college and get a great job soon after. I was going to get that upgrade in salary, pay off my debts, and start building a life of fulfillment.

Then COVID hit, and things shifted.

I covered exactly one day of the Big Ten Tournament before its cancellation. I attended online classes to finish my semester and graduated. Six months later, I am still running produce at Walmart. My salary has not changed and under the standards of societal expectations, I am probably falling behind or underachieving.

I let those societal expectations get to me for a while. Then I thought—*a lot*—and realized that I'm doing just fine. Now I'm writing a book to explain why.

Maybe the book is for you—a fellow 20-something that feels lost and needs some guidance. Maybe you are a teenager wondering how your next 10-15 years might end up. Maybe you are 30 or older and want to tell me my outlook is correct (or wrong). Maybe I'm writing it for myself to feel better.

Either way, we're going to dig into my mind and see just what the hell I think creates happiness and fulfillment while dispelling some myths that society forces down our throats as soon as we're old enough to understand language.

Let's enjoy this journey together.

Dylan Hughes, November, 22, 2020

CHAPTER 1: LOSING YOURSELF IN SOMEBODY ELSE

Ah yes, every good man's famous last words: "Well, I think I like a girl."

My history with girls is checkered at best. I was "in love" with the girl across the street for a good 10 years, and she didn't like me back. I liked a few girls in high school that didn't like me back. I liked a few girls in college that didn't like me back. As a junior in college, I entered into my first relationship. It lasted six weeks.

It was fun and it ended on good terms. It also showed me that I was probably better off being single anyway.

I've always been somewhat introverted in that I really enjoy time to myself. I don't like to call myself introverted because I'm not super shy and I do like being around other people. But I value my alone time quite a bit.

When dating someone, you don't get as much of that. Lesson learned!

For about a year and a half, I got back to being the me I had always been: a lone wolf working towards his goals of becoming a professional sports writer (or a professional writer of any sort, really).

Then, I met a girl.

I had told myself ever since I started working that I didn't want to date a girl I worked with. It's a lot easier to tell yourself that when you haven't actually met a girl you like at work. Once I did, I threw that idea right out the window.

For a couple months, I didn't talk to this girl but once. Like many people I work with, we just walked by each other, did our jobs, and went home. She was just another face in the crowd, albeit a very cute face.

One day, I felt the urge to compliment her hair, which was different that day than usual. I did so and she thanked me although didn't seem to think much of it. I put my head down and got back to work.

Not long after that, she was near me and started asking me questions about myself. I knew at that point that she was interested.

For the following couple of weeks, we chatted here and there but nothing more. I came in on a Sunday after a previously-scheduled plan fell through and we ended up working with each other for a few hours. The next day, she followed me on Instagram.

We exchanged messages for a couple days before she gave me her number. We then started texting a lot and it moved pretty quickly.

Not long after we started texting, we both acknowledged that we liked each other. It wasn't that serious. Well, maybe on her end, at least. I had pretty quickly fallen in that damned hole.

I got to a bad place—a place where I worried if she wasn't texting me, she was texting someone else. I worried about the future—if she wouldn't commit to me, would she find someone else in the meantime?

I overlooked the fact that despite texting for months on end, every single day, we only hung out outside of work *once*. I gave her a break—she did work *three* jobs after all.

For the majority of spring and the entirety of summer, I was in pain. I went home from work and was stuck in my head all day. I'd tie myself to my phone and connect my mood to the mood of the conversation. Looking back at that version of myself, it's almost as if my soul was floating around my body rather than within it. I was not who I had always been.

A girl had never made me feel that way before, but it took me a while to realize a girl should never make me feel *that* way. I rarely felt good. I was always uneasy, always hoping she would come around, and never addressed the concerning red flags that were apparent on a daily basis.

I got caught up in the idea rather than the reality. I had always craved a committed relationship and that little, tiny connection I had with this girl gave me a taste of that. But that taste was bitter, and the bitterness sent me down a road I never intend to go down again.

After months of swimming in my pool of agony, I was able to confront the issues and move on. I realized that she would always find an excuse not to commit—to a date, let alone a relationship. I realized that she valued my company but only when it was good for her. I realized that the suffering I put myself through would have no end if I kept going down that road.

After all, *I* was putting myself through this, not her. I allowed her actions to harm me, and giving someone that kind of control was no longer something I was willing to allow.

This story does have a point: value your mental health and happiness over everything. If a person (or thing) is causing you pain, remove them. You and only you are able to change your environment to improve your life.

This story is important as it is a foundation for the house I have built—or begun building—in the months following its closure. Thanks to the lessons I learned from this experience, I have become obsessed with happiness, purpose/meaning, and everything that comes along with it. And in just a few months time, I have a few experiences that have given me the initial bricks for my current mental home.

CHAPTER 2: THE NEVER-ENDING SELF-IMPROVEMENT GAME

After months of soaking in anger, sadness, and pity, I rebounded *quickly*. Or tried to, at least.

Turning to the self-improvement machine after going through a failed mission is about as natural of an instinct as there is. Hating your situation only lasts for so long before bad thoughts start turning *really* bad. If you don't want to get to that really bad place, where do you turn?

Motivational YouTube!

Ah, YouTube…what a great place. One or two keywords get you exactly where you want to be. Typing in "motivation" brings up the likes of David Goggins, Tony Robbins, Gary Vaynerchuk, and Joe Rogan—laying out the blueprint for flipping the script on your unfulfilling life.

Making changes is easy at first. To dig myself out of the hole, I started waking up between 5 and 6 a.m. everyday and going for a run. As I ran around my city with no cars on the road and no lights on in houses, I felt great. While everybody was sleeping, I was accomplishing something.

Exercise is probably the best way to get yourself out of a rut. Exercising is easier for some and harder for others. For people like me, who like exercising, pushing myself to the limits and breaking through personal barriers is a great feeling. It's not super difficult to rev myself up and challenge myself to break a personal record. When I do it, I feel awesome and look forward to continuing to push myself. When I don't, well, at least I tried.

The people that don't like exercising have even more to gain from it. If you get up early and go for a run, or do any sort of exercise throughout the day, you have proven that you can motivate yourself internally and accomplish things you truly hate to do. Whether you are going hard or going light, it's better than doing nothing.

In August of 2020, I competed in a challenge on Nike Run Club and placed in the top 20% of competitors, running over 70 miles that month. Within that month I broke personal records such as longest run by distance (6.25 miles), longest run in time (1:00:31), and fastest 10K (1:00:03).

Since that month, I have run a total of nine miles.

While the running and idea of rabid improvement excited me in the beginning of August, I realized by the end that it could only do so much for me. It was a great way to clear my head and help me focus on what I really loved doing: writing. Pushing myself to finish in the top 10% of the challenge kept me going. Even though I fell short, I was proud to run 70 miles in a month and finish above 80% of the runners participating.

After that was behind me, though, I didn't feel like I needed to run anymore. It made me feel good and healthy, but I realized I wasn't going to change my life and shed my past sadness by running problems out through my shoes. It was going to take deliberate daily actions to focus on what made me happy.

While running wasn't the answer, it did teach me a lot. One of the goals of keeping to my running plan was to learn discipline and the power of sticking to something.

A key pillar in many of these motivational YouTube videos is the idea of small, incremental improvements. Building positive daily habits into your life can help you grow into a superhuman of sorts. Even small actions can build up to something marvelous if they are performed everyday.

In the month of August, my schedule was fairly rigid. On days that I worked, I woke up early, ran, ate a good breakfast, worked, and came home to work on my writing. I did the same thing on days I didn't work—minus the work, of course.

Having a defined schedule felt good as it wasn't as easy to wander mindlessly as it is with a loose, undefined schedule. During those months of waiting around the phone all day for texts from the girl, I had few things to distract me and keep my mind busy. I sat around most of the days thinking, which was very bad for me.

With things to do, though, it wasn't as easy for my mind to go into that bad place.

While I don't wake up early and run anymore, I still try to have a relatively defined schedule. I don't think about girls much in my freetime, but a loose schedule can still lead to thinking about worthless things and feeling relatively uneasy. Rest is a necessary thing for our body and mind, but too much rest can lead to a feeling of uselessness. Having a passion project of sorts, whether it's a job, sidegig, or fun hobby, keeps you balanced and happy.

Rabid self-improvement is more of a journey than a destination. You are coming from a place of anger, sadness, humility, and failure, looking to open a door into a brighter personal universe. The lessons you learn during that phase are that those measures to improve yourself are not sustainable as your sole meaning for waking up. They become sustainable once they are built into a schedule filled with passionate work and spending time with loved ones.

If you love exercising and find it best to wake up super early to do so, do that so long as your heart desires. But just know that becoming shredded won't make you happy, and your ruthless effort to fill that pit with dirt won't be successful if you're digging new holes in the process.

CHAPTER 3: FINDING A JOB IS TOUGHER THAN IT SEEMS

Finding a job in the journalism field is tougher than I thought.

Back in high school, I always looked forward to my college graduation day. At that time, as a 16-17-year-old kid, I thought I was something special. I started writing at a young age (14 or so) and was ahead of the pack. The competition I'd one day face in the job market didn't have the advantage I had: time and experience. By the time I'd be graduating college, I'd have a book full of connections, recommendations, and published stories. I'd have no problem getting a job, and really, I should have no problem getting a job before I even get my degree.

The closer I got to that coveted graduation day, the less confident I was in my post-graduate job prospects.

By the time I got to college, the vast majority of my writing portfolio was made up of online sports blogging with a couple handfuls of high school newspaper clippings mixed in. College was the perfect opportunity to beef up my portfolio and diversify it a bit with better developed stories—and perhaps even some non-sports writing.

In my first year of college, I didn't have many opportunities to get stories done as I was attending community college. Well, that's what I told myself, anyways. A true journalist can find a story anywhere, and I guess I didn't fit the "true journalist" bill back then.

Once I got to IUPUI, one of the most dedicated sports journalism programs in the country, it was going to be easy to get opportunities. It wouldn't take long for me to start grabbing the attention of job recruiters everywhere.

In my first two years at IUPUI, my sophomore and junior years, I didn't do much of anything to bolster my portfolio. I continued blogging about sports, but it became clear to me in my junior year that sports writing likely wasn't going to be my path to success in the writing world.

It turns out, there are thousands of kids my age that also think writing about sports for a living would be pretty cool and are pursuing it at the same time as me. In a world where advertising agencies are spending less and less on media, newsrooms are shrinking and the field is heading towards becoming completely freelance.

In my senior year, I got tons of experience—because, well, I had no choice if I hoped to become anything. I got published in a large local magazine (through my internship), covered multiple professional sporting events, interviewed professional and collegiate coaches and athletes, and even covered some campus interests for the student newspaper.

In May of 2020, I became a college graduate. Instead of trading my degree in for a professional byline at some esteemed media outlet, I threw it on my dresser and got ready to go run some produce at the job I worked at throughout college (and planned to quit long ago).

For a while, it was kind of nice to have the COVID excuse. When people asked about my job search, I told them, "Well, companies are being tight right now with the virus going around. It may take a while to find something."

Even now, six months after my graduation, COVID is the excuse.

It's not an excuse I use anymore, though. Without even prompting it, friends and family will bring it up as an excuse for my failure to find a professional writing job, whether I agree with that being the reason or not.

I'll admit it: I haven't tried *that* hard to find a job. I'm picky and not willing to take some rinky-dink writing gig for a small outlet that will pay me what I'm making now as a produce associate working 30 hours a week. I know exactly what will happen if I start writing about boring ass subjects five days a week for a paycheck: I will start to hate writing. I know because I've done it before.

Writing is what I love to do. I've known that I wanted to be a professional writer since I was in fourth grade. How many people can say they discovered their passion when they were still in elementary school?

Some people say you have to channel your inner child to discover what really makes you happy, and I did that exercise with my writing. Why did I love writing at such a young age? Well, there was probably something subconscious in me that has drawn me to this medium, like my curiosity, love for story-telling, and teaching others on topics I'm passionate about.

Actually, you know, maybe that was all conscious, too. I liked making up stories and turning a blank page into something fun and interesting. That has stuck with me to this day.

I turned on email notifications for countless job sites and visited Indeed and the LinkedIn job section as often as I could throughout the summer. Again, I was picky, so I only applied for 10-15 jobs. But I worked for hours to perfect my cover letter and resume and sought my favorite and most reputable professor to write me a stunning recommendation.

Guess what? Only one of my applications received a response. The rest fell into the pile of rejections without even just a one-sentence email to let me know that I should look elsewhere for work.

After carefully selecting and applying for these jobs for months, I gave up in August and created my business newsletter, "Heavy Pockets," through Substack. In September, I began writing consistently on Medium.com.

I have always wanted to be my own boss. I've never hated a boss, but I hated the idea of working towards someone else's goals. At my current job, I work towards the sales and profit goals of my employer. The work I do, good or bad, doesn't change the amount of money added to my bank account every two weeks. Working my butt off equates to more profit for them and nothing but time and effort spent for me.

This is something I've had a problem with for a long time. As mentioned earlier, I have worked this job throughout the majority of my college tenure. As of this writing, I have worked there for over three and a half years. The greatest lesson I have taken away from this job is that I don't want this kind of job. I want a job where my effort earns me a larger piece of the pie.

As a writer, I am naturally attracted to projects. I enjoy working at something big over time, celebrating when it's over, and moving on to the next thing. I don't enjoy working hard to finish tasks one day only to have to do the same exact thing the next day.

Would writing for some small paper that pays $20,000 a year allow me some freedom to write about what I want and give me something different to do every day? Sure, most likely. Would that allow me to get the entry-level experience I need to move up to a larger media outlet in two or three years? Probably. But is any of that worth it?

I am not naive enough to believe my writing is going to change the world and therefore should be valued at a high rate. I understand how the world works: experience equals monetary value and I don't have much. When I apply for a cool sports writing job in Texas or Georgia, they throw me into the pile of other recently-graduated journalism students looking to get their feet wet. We just don't do it for them.

I know I'm a good writer, though, and can offer value to people if I focus my attention in the right areas. That's why I took matters into my own hands by creating my newsletter and joining Medium.

Both of these decisions were made knowing I was potentially missing out on working as a copywriter or internal communications writer for some local firm, and therefore, cash in the bank. I also knew that I'd likely be stuck in my current job or a similar job to cover my expenses until I "got my big break."

These were things I became comfortable with after discovering what I really wanted out of life.

Writing for a company is great: you get a salary, benefits, and experience to carry with you to your next job and the one after that. In exchange for those gains, you have to abide by their editorial standards, write what they want you to write, and sacrifice your passion projects to help the company reach its bottom line.

Don't get it twisted: whether it's in retail or media, companies are trying to make money. Your purpose is to make them money—and they are making more money from your work than they are paying you.

Not everyone realizes this, and the ones that do can only care so much because they need a paycheck. As a 23-year-old with supportive parents (a.k.a ones that don't make me pay rent) and very few liabilities to my name, however, I'm able to focus on what I want rather than what I need.

What I want is to write what I want to write about, where I want to write, and make all the money from the content (well, what's left after the platforms take their small cut). If it fails and I don't make much, oh well. I will have hundreds of stories to take to those same media companies down the road.

I hope it doesn't get to that, though. I didn't think I'd be writing this book a couple weeks ago and here we are. I already have an idea for another book. I'm a writer and I need to write. And for the life of me, I hope it's for myself and not some company.

CHAPTER 4: GETTING MORE FROM LESS THROUGH MINIMALISM

What if less actually *was* more?

As kids, we heard this saying all the time. But most of us were probably too dumb to figure out what the hell it meant.

For the past three years, I've been focusing on *more*. I became an investor in the stock market in late 2017 hoping to get rich. I wanted *more* money so I could buy *more* things. And not just regular things—expensive things.

For the longest time, my mind was fixated on living a life of luxury. It wasn't necessarily to impress other people; I just liked nice things. I loved Audis. I wanted to collect expensive Nike shoes. I wanted nice houses in cool cities. I wanted all the latest technology. More, more, more.

There was a reason I was like this: I didn't grow up with many nice things. Well, not as much as the kids I was friends with and went to school with, at least.

We weren't poor or even broke, but we were tight on money a lot of the time. For the majority of my childhood, my dad carried a heavy load, working long hours in factories to make ends meet.

My mom had collected quite a long list of medical issues over the years, with most coming from a bad car accident that made it very hard for her to work. The burden grew on my dad.

You know how some people say, "If you were broke but didn't know it, you had great parents"? I don't think that's fair. My brother and I knew we had money issues, but that didn't mean our parents were doing a bad job. It was hard to hide. But it was OK: it made it easier to cope with the fact that we didn't have what our well-off peers had.

And even with our financial struggles, our parents did a great job of giving us *something* each year. While we didn't have a hundred presents under the Christmas tree or lavish vacations every year, we did fun things a handful of times each year and got great quality time with our parents.

Each year, my dad would take me to the Indianapolis 500—a tradition that has lived on since I first went during the third grade (up until this year; thanks, COVID). He would take my brother and I to car shows or air shows each year, too. It wasn't that dream Florida vacation, but it was enough.

While I appreciated these moments, I also realized as I got older that I didn't want my kids to go 18 years before boarding a plane with their parents for the first time to go on a nice vacation. I didn't want them to feel like they weren't getting as much on Christmas as their peers.

I remember even just a couple years ago on our trip to Treasure Island, FL. At this point, my parents were long past their financial struggles, and we could afford to go on a decent vacation every year. After months of research, my mom came across this little vacation town not too far from St. Petersburg.

This wasn't our first time going to Florida together. A year and a half prior, we went to Panama City Beach and had an awesome time. It was the perfect beach, the perfect weather, and the perfect condo. Every beach vacation I would take from then on would be compared to that.

Well, compared to PCB, Treasure Island *sucked*. The beaches weren't as nice. Our condo wasn't as nice. The weather sucked. It was fairly disappointing.

One night, as I sat on our balcony and looked off into the dark abyss that is the ocean without sunlight, I started thinking. "This is *exactly* why I need to be rich. My kids won't have vacations that suck."

I don't know whether I was blaming my parents for choosing a bad vacation destination, the rain taking away from our beach time, or if I was just being an asshole, but...

Actually, no. I was just being an asshole.

Either way, that's where my mind was at. I was still focused on *more*.

And where did this mindset get me? As my family (and friend we brought along) was enjoying one of our handful of evenings away from boring Indiana life, drinking and listening to music, my mind was elsewhere. I was looking towards a future I was so far away from instead of focusing on what I had right in front of me: a loving support group that was just taking it easy.

In the two-plus years since then, but mostly in the past six or so months, I've been able to realize the benefits of being able to appreciate less. Less doesn't equal lack. It doesn't take lots of money and stuff to be happy. Sustainable happiness is generated from being able to support yourself, having supportive friends and family, and doing fulfilling work. Anything more is gravy.

I'm not going to look back on that night in Florida and say what I *should* have done, because hindsight is 20/20. It was a lesson I had to learn. But I will say that, on future vacations, I will *not* be thinking about how to make those moments better in the future.

All we have is now.

Growing up the way I did provided me with the perfect level of perspective to confidently move forward in my life. My parents weren't perfect with their money back then and still aren't now. They weren't perfect in other ways, too.

But isn't that the point? You will naturally make mistakes—as a parent, child, sibling, and friend. As a parent, you turn those mistakes into lessons for your kid. And if you aren't able to do it, maybe they'll carry it with them and figure it out on their own later in life. Sometimes it's even better that way.

As we grew up tight on cash week-to-week while the city around us thrived, it showed me both sides of the coin. On one side, you could be working your ass off every week having to support a family of four, making sure to get food on the table, but not sure if all of the bills would be paid on time. It's a revolving door of stress that eventually weighs on the psyche of a person.

On the other side, you see your friends getting cool toys and going on trips once or twice a year. You see that life of (perceived) limited stress and want it for yourself.

This perspective of clashing lifestyles is easily seen in my financial habits nowadays. I rarely spend money on non-essential items, saving or investing whatever is left over after my bills are paid.

To be honest, I kind of hate *stuff* at this point. What is *stuff* to people anyway? One of the things I never got jealous of was my friends getting new iPhones every year or worthless upgrades to any kind of electronics, really. Getting new clothes when they already have a closet full. Even as a teenager, before entering my *turns ego dial to max* current state of wisdom, I recognized how dumb it was to spend money on these things.

My spending habits are much more tailored to my needs than I would have hoped for as a younger kid. Whether I am rich or not, I have a hard time seeing myself putting out for a slightly-upgraded phone every year—or even every two years—when that model made four years ago still works and is cheap as hell.

Just recently, the next-generation gaming consoles came out and everyone is trying to grab them. They are flying off the (virtual) shelves so quickly that websites are sold out almost instantly. Admittedly, I hoped to grab one, and would have had the demand not been so high.

After thinking, though, I realized how making that purchase went against everything I stood for. The console I currently own has been solid for eight years without a single issue. Why not ride it for as long as possible?

Anyone can justify making a purchase. You can convince yourself that spending on this or that is a good idea because you *need* it. But what you actually need is much less than what you think.

That's what minimalism is all about. It's not necessarily about less (or lack), it's just about focusing on what you truly need. This can mean cleaning up your email inbox (digital minimalism), cleaning out your closet, or selling/donating that box of electronics that you spent hundreds of dollars on and barely use. It could mean doing none of that but changing how you spend your money moving forward.

Start saving/investing that money you spend each month on *wants* and re-prioritize. What do you actually need? What makes you happy? The answers are easier to find than you may think. You just have to move all that excess stuff out of the way first.

CHAPTER 5: THE PRESSURE TO STAY BUSY

"It's not that you have a lot to do. It's that you're being defined by a constant reactive comparison."

Those are the words of Greg McKeown, author of "Essentialism: The Disciplined Pursuit of Less," in an interview with minimalist YouTuber Matt D'Avella.

First of all, you may be getting confused now. While minimalism and essentialism may sound like different things, they are really one in the same. So don't trip up over dumb terminology.

Second of all, you may be seeing a pattern in my thinking now. When discussing the idea of less, it can be easy to miss things. "Less money and stuff = more time and freedom" is the general way people see minimalism.

Really, though, it's a lot deeper than that.

Minimalism (and essentialism) focus on significance, importance, and value. While that focus ultimately leads to fewer possessions, it is not aimed solely at eliminating material items from your life. It is aimed at getting use and value out of everything you own, and significance and fulfillment from everything you do.

One of the main enemies of the minimalist lifestyle is "hustle culture." Hustle culture is the product of the promotion of *doing more*. Most of the time, but not all the time, this promotion has little guidance and gives the impression that hard work leads to success *no matter what.*

For a moment, think to yourself: do you think hard work leads to success, no matter what you are working on?

Hard work does of course lead to success. No superstar athlete got to where he or she is by skipping the gym and eating poorly. No business founder reached the top by skipping networking events and missing important client meetings.

Those people got to where they are by working hard on the right things—not just by working hard.

Many people take pride in hard work, and that's understandable. Blue collar work is quite literally *hard* work. It's hard to survive in those lines of work by being lazy. A construction worker being lackadaisical while nailing boards together or a landscaper skipping the weed-whacking gets fired.

Taking pride in blue collar work is respectable, so long as you find true fulfillment in the work. If you find true joy in building homes from the ground up or fixing furnaces for a family of four in the middle of winter, that is wonderful. You can go home at night feeling that your work was truly worthwhile and that your hard work has paid off.

There are certainly people like that—people that go home feeling tired but also truly happy inside. And there are just as many people, but likely more, that go home feeling pride simply because they worked hard.

You may think, "What's the difference? They feel prideful either way." The truth is that "hard work pride" fades over time. In my experience, at least.

Hard work does feel good for some time. Going home tired shows that you did your part and earned your money for that day. When you inevitably face challenges in your work, though, you will start to ask yourself, "What is this even for?"

In my time working as a cog in the big retail machine, I have certainly had days where I was proud of the work I put in. I went home too tired to do anything else, but at least I worked hard today, right?

Then come the bad days, where you want to go home and do something else but have to stay over to cover for someone else's mistakes (or pure laziness). You have to work your butt off so your employer can reap the rewards while your reward is...a feeling of accomplishment? For working hard?

What is that feeling truly worth? Do you really want to make your work a consistent paycheck and nothing else to show for it but a *feeling*?

It is hard to simply *not* work hard, though, because everyone else around us does. If we don't work as hard as Harry or Sally, we are lazy and should feel worthless.

This is an idea Tim Kreider touches on in his 2012 New York Times piece entitled, "The 'Busy' Trap."

In this piece, Kreider explains the busyness epidemic in America, where people stay busy simply to...stay busy.

"They're busy because of their own ambition or drive or anxiety, because they're addicted to busyness and dread what they might have to face in its absence," Kreider writes.

While it is useless for me to determine the most important chapter of this book (that is up to you), I believe this is a central theme for the book, and ties the previous chapter on minimalism and future chapters on comparison and identity together well.

As humans, it is natural for us to constantly evaluate where we are, question our self-worth, and ponder the meaning of our individual lives and humanity as a whole. Being productive helps answer a lot of these questions and fill our self-created "holes."

Again, though: what is the point of being productive if it isn't actually getting us anywhere?

In "Essentialism," Greg McKeown discusses the uselessness of spreading ourselves so thin and pulling ourselves in so many different directions. It's hard to see the momentum in our lives that motivates us to continue when we are fragmenting our focus so much.

Think of it like digging holes. If you dig in the same spot everyday, you will eventually get to your destination far beneath the surface. If you dig a little bit in a bunch of different spots, however, it's going to take you ages to get deeper than surface level.

When we can tell people that we are doing this, that, and the other, though, it reflects our wide range of skills, abilities, and usefulness. Our ability to make a significant impact in any one thing becomes severely limited when we are spreading our attention so thin, however.

Here's another example. I am currently writing this book. I have at least one more idea for another book. If I began working on that book now, though, it would be hard for me to put the proper research and thought behind *either* book. Flipping your brain back and forth between two different projects can be confusing. Good, useful ideas could be forgotten or underdeveloped.

Being busy is OK. Just stay busy doing the right things. Don't fill your schedule up for the sake of having something to do. Fill your schedule up with activities that will positively contribute to what truly matters to you.

And what people around us are doing should not impact what we do or how we go about things.

My ultimate hope for this chapter—and book as a whole—is that you find that thing to finally fill the emptiness in your heart. I want you to realize that the fulfillment you seek comes from within, not from without. Being happy is staying true to yourself —filling your needs and not your wants.

The truth is, you will always *want* more, but you will rarely *need* more. Make it easy on yourself.

CHAPTER 6: OVERTHINKING IS PERSONAL ENSLAVEMENT

Have you ever actively sat around and analyzed what your brain thinks about?

That thing is an absolute nut job.

I think one of the most important steps in achieving a higher level of happiness is the realization that you are not what you think about. Your brain is constantly going—analyzing situations, relationships, and future plans. It worries about things out of your control, it creates situations that aren't real, and it starts planning for things that aren't viable yet.

Here's an idea: stop thinking about all that. Focus on right now and right now alone.

I want to make it clear that this is *not* easy. This is something that requires almost constant action. Thoughts come and go. How far they go is up to you.

I also want to make it clear that I am not very good at this yet. I still catch my mind wandering and focusing on things out of my current self's control. Thanks to actively confronting my thoughts over the past few months, though, I am in a lot better of a place.

I will walk through some examples in my life. But because of my lack of experience, I will also detail some more experienced accounts I have discovered.

Just to get this out of the way, let's talk about the girl from Chapter 1 again.

The sole reason I got to such a bad place mentally while talking to this girl was the creation of expectations and fake events in my head.

As previously mentioned, I worked about half as much as this girl did in a day/week, so I did a lot of sitting around while she was occupied. I became a slave to my phone as my attention was solely on her and maintaining an active text conversation. Texting was all I had with her. When she texted, I wanted to respond in a timely manner. While I waited for a response, I sat around thinking.

Some of this thinking was on my back patio. I love my back patio. During those nice, summer days, I lounged back on a comfy chair, taking in all the nature around me. Trees taller than my house, birds buzzing around, squirrels treading on skimpy branches, and of course, the family of three Huskies that live catty corner to my family.

Current Me misses those warm, summer nights where I had the pleasure of spending an evening in nature. Now, in December, I spend as much time away from the damn cold as I can.

Current Me doesn't miss those specific nights, though. Instead of living in nature, living in the moment and appreciating what was surrounding me and taking account of the good things in my life, I lived in my head, focusing on what I didn't have: her.

My mind was constantly flickering back and forth between the nature of my surroundings and the nature of my thoughts. I was able to sit and think about how cool nature really is. How all these animals in my backyard live off instinct, building homes in trees and fending for themselves. I observed my dog staring off into the distance, reacting to any noise he heard, envious of the simple life he lived.

It took me until months after those nights to realize I could live a simple life like him.

Well, not *exactly* like him. The dude sleeps, begs for food, plays, and barks at cute squirrels, all day, every day. Humans, by nature, don't have it that easy.

These things all tie back together, though. It seems as though every species but human can focus on needs instead of wants. Dogs need sleep, food, love, and purpose (yes, I am convinced my dog's purpose is to protect our backyard from rodents). That's all we need, yet we constantly seek more.

Anyways, that's beside the point I am trying to make.

Aside from analyzing nature, I'd read, watch YouTube videos, and write way less than I should have. Looking back, however, I believe I was simply trying to distract myself from thinking about this girl. I was so far separated from myself, I still can't believe it.

These evenings were full of reflection, oftentimes over the same things. I would analyze text conversations, how I let it get like that, if things would ever change, what my breaking point would be. I'd go on long bike rides, too, thinking over the same points. My mind became a treadmill of sad thoughts.

Not thinking about people is easier than it sounds. I have always maintained a small circle. When I open myself up to the idea of letting someone new in, I view them in a completely different light than most other people. I become vulnerable to very few people. I am nice and energized around people that I know on a surface level. But they never get 100% of me.

Taking that leap means a lot. When that person doesn't accept entry into my tight circle, it hurts. It's hard to just let that go.

You may not be able to relate to this at all. You may have a very easy time cutting people off and forgetting about them. If that is you, I envy you tremendously. That is not me, though, and never will be. So I have to find a different way to handle things.

To be honest, this girl does still enter my mind quite often. It's just the nature of it. Again, I am not an expert of killing useless thinking. But I am trying and improving.

The first step to ridding yourself of these thoughts is to actually address that they are happening. Your mind is constantly going and it won't be stopped unless you make an effort to stop it. It's very easy to let it run its mouth all day because you just become used to it. Once you start viewing your thoughts from more of an outside perspective, it becomes easier to mute those inner comments.

Once you start confronting your thoughts, ask yourself, "Is this a thought worth acknowledging? Is this something I can control?" For me, the answers to both of those questions were no.

While I have always been good at not worrying whether people like me or not, it is certainly more difficult when it comes to girls. Like I said, if I am willing to open myself up to the idea of letting this person into my life and they turn away from it, it sends me into evaluation mode.

It took me a long time to learn that this evaluation is useless.

For handling this specific situation, I would recommend looking at it this way. She doesn't like you. Did you do anything crazy or dumb to turn her off? If yes, apologize for that, try to fix it, and try again. If she simply didn't like you because of you, move on. Why would you like someone that doesn't like you?

This is easier said than done, I know. But running through situations in your head about why she may not like you or want to be with you is not constructive. Hell, you could even straight-up ask her why she doesn't want to be with you if that makes it easier. But if you don't want to do that or it's not possible, evaluate your approach, her response, learn from it, and move on.

Overthinking will lead you to the despair that I fell into—focusing my energy on someone that didn't want to be with me, who also never proved herself as a worthy partner. A small percentage of my feelings towards her were based on reality; the rest came from the *idea* of a relationship with her that was created in my head.

If the thoughts are not actionable or help with present goals, I start thinking of something else. I start thinking of story ideas or maybe even focus on the positive things going on in my life.

I'll let you hear it from someone else as well. Anthony Metivier, a memory trainer, did a Tedx Talk on the process of silencing negative thoughts. Or as he poignantly calls it, "Blah blah blah blah blah."

Metivier discussed what he learned from Gary Weber, author of books "Happiness Beyond Thought" and "Evolving Beyond Thought." In these books, according to Metivier, Weber recommends memorizing ancient Sanskrit writing that is designed to help cut through the thoughts of our wandering mind.

There were two questions in the Sanskrit that Metivier mentioned: "Are my thoughts useful? How do they behave?"

This falls in line with my (long-winded) example. While I wasn't asking these exact questions, I was asking something similar. The more you do it, the more the thoughts start to fade away.

There is a quote from Eckhart Tolle, author of "The Power of Now," that sums this all up perfectly: "What a liberation to realize that the 'voice in my head' is not who I am. Who am I then? The one who sees that."

Much, if not all, of Tolle's experience in enlightenment comes from the principles of Buddhism. "To desire is to suffer" is a Buddhist idea that Tolle discusses in "The Power of Now."

"All cravings are the mind seeking salvation or fulfillment in external things and in the future as a substitute for the joy of Being. As long as I am my mind, I am those cravings, those needs, wants, attachments, and aversions, and apart from them there is no 'I' except as a mere possibility, an unfulfilled potential, a seed that has not yet sprouted."

This is an incredibly powerful observation that took me multiple readings to fully digest. The fact that external occurrences don't give us joy, simply pleasure, is not a new or under-discussed topic. It is hard to imagine a person that hasn't at least heard of this concept, whether they believe it to be true or not.

It is undeniable that our identity, which I will discuss more later on, is made up of just what Tolle mentioned: our needs, wants, attachments, and aversions. Much of "The Power of Now" comes from a spiritual standpoint, which I don't plan on touching here. Without those cravings, as Tolle said, we are not who we are. While stripping those away would reveal our true, spiritual Being, those cravings make up our earthly selves and that's what I am focusing on here.

These cravings are a product of our mind, though. They are not a product of our true, conscious self. Their revelations through our thinking will not always accurately represent our true selves. We are what we do, not what we think.

There are two important things to take away here: desire is suffering but to be human is to desire. Therefore, you should desire.

What you *should* desire becomes the question. When you are in a state of desire, you are disturbing your inner peace. When desiring, ask yourself, "Can I get back to my inner peace through this desire? Is this desire capable of delivering me to a higher place of happiness or will I return to my current state?"

The answers to these questions, of course, are subjective. Each person's joy comes from different sources. But we now know that external materials and recognition won't equal joy (long-term), simply pleasure (short-term). Dig deep to find the source.

We overweight our thoughts. Because they come from within, we assume they are truth. But they are not. The ones who realize that will find that next level of happiness.

The tidiness of our mind matters more than anything. No matter where you live, what you achieve, or who you know, your head will always be home. Turn the noise down on the useless thoughts and amplify the useful ones.

CHAPTER 7: COMPARISON WILL CAUSE SUFFERING

For the next handful of pages, I will be re-purposing an article I recently wrote on the crushing expectations of society entitled, "Overachieving is Not a Necessity." After that, I will delve deeper into comparison and its harmful nature.

We are living in a culture of numbers. The amount of money you make matters. The number of friends you have matters. The number of accomplishments you have matters.

Well, they matter to the people viewing your life from an outside perspective. But they shouldn't matter to you.

Many people fall into the trap of comparing themselves to the standards of society. "What most people do is what I should do. If not, I am a failure."

This is toxic thinking and can disease your mind and hurt your mentality moving forward.

Reaching the standards of society, or slightly finishing above the pack, is great for some people. These standards are things like making a lot of money and having a lot of friends. For some, this is happiness. And that's great!

But different things make different people happy and the truly unique individuals in the world don't fall into the numbers trap.

Individuals should be focusing on impactfulness over abundance.

Making a lot of money has its upsides — it provides security and can allow you to purchase things and experiences you enjoy. Having a lot of friends also has upsides — knowing more people gives you more opportunities to do fun things.

There are also major downsides to focusing on "having more," however.
Making more money often comes at the cost of time — whether it be time in your day or even time in your life (stress kills!). If you are not happy doing the job that nets this high income, is it really worth it?

Having more friends can also cost precious time and mental clarity. Knowing more people opens you up to more deception, anger, and stress. At the end of the day, some people are very self-centered, and they will not flinch to hurt or deceive you if it helps them in any way. You shouldn't be afraid to filter out the bad eggs, even if it means fewer fun opportunities.

There is an overall pressure in society to do more. Once you accomplish one goal, it's time to move to the next.

Over time, this kind of behavior leaves us ungrateful and always looking to the next thing. If we are not able to reflect on one accomplishment (or failure) before moving on, it will have been a wasted feat. Racking up wins is undoubtedly positive, but along with those wins comes lessons. Taking time to soak in and understand why or how something happened gives us a blueprint for the next challenge.

Constantly looking to achieve also makes it harder to simply appreciate these accomplishments.

The goal should be to seek fulfillment over achievement. Less can be more if your actions have meaning and your goals have purpose.

Fulfillment can't be measured in numbers. Making less money and having fewer friends can absolutely equate to a happier life, so long as your personal standard for living is met and fulfilled.

The lesson is simple: the mean of society doesn't actually represent the average standards of its people. You are your own person; follow your heart's map and find your personal standard for happiness.

Measurement in any form can drag us down because it gives us an expectation. This is another form of the external seekings that I discussed in the previous chapter.

The problem with what is given is that it can be taken back. Words of praise can be countered by words of disdain. An action that is lauded can be wrong and an action that is hated could be right. The only respected source of approval or disapproval should come from within. Find peace in what you do and the opinions of others will fall on deaf ears.

After reading the early chapters of "The Power of Now," I went into another level of dissecting my hopes and dreams. Obviously, I want to be able to support myself as a writer. I have never really set a specific amount I'd like to earn or a certain amount of followers I'd like to gain. I have always focused on simply getting to the point of self-sustainability.

A few months back, when I began the journey that I am currently on, I was focused on achieving these goals through Medium—a self-publishing site that pays writers for the amount of time readers spend on articles.

In my first month writing "full-time" on Medium, I earned $3.73. In the second month, I earned $6.95. In my third month, I earned

$11.94.

My hope is to get close to doubling the prior month's earnings every month. At that rate, I'd be earning $100 in about three months. I'd be earning $1,000 in seven months.

These are numbers I can only project and not control, of course. The only thing I can control is my output.

While I will probably never reach the Zen status of Tolle, I can do my best to focus only on what I can control.

I view this book in the same way. A past version of myself would love to get rich off of a book, especially the first one I publish, and see it impact millions of people. I have little control on its reach, how it impacts people, and their ultimate word of mouth after it is published, though. I can only control the writing within and however I may choose to share it in the future.

Once this book is written, edited, and distributed, the focus will not be on numbers. I will sell it cheaply in hopes of the message reaching as many people as possible. I will wish for its message to help people. Whether they feel compelled enough to share it is up to them.

I try to focus on what I give rather than what I receive anymore. What can I give? Writing, in the form of a book or article, is what I can give. What I receive is up to the world and will not be a focus of my process.

You may think, "How can you not care about the success of your work? How can you sustain yourself without reaching for as many dollars as possible?"

Faith.

Faith in our process is all we have. Again, I *do* want these writings to reach large numbers of people, but the only thing I can do to achieve that is write useful words and hope people find them. If that doesn't happen, I will continue to try.

A simple quote from Hall of Fame football coach Bill Walsh sticks with me when thinking of these types of pursuits: "The score takes care of itself."

There is a much longer quote from Tolle that essentially says the same thing.

"So do not be concerned with the fruit of your action — just give attention to the action itself. The fruit will come of its own accord. This is a powerful spiritual practice. In the Bhagavad Gita, one of the oldest and most beautiful spiritual teachings in existence, nonattachment to the fruit of your action is called Karma Yoga. It is described as the path of "consecrated action." When the compulsive striving away from the Now ceases, the joy of Being flows into everything you do. The moment your attention turns to the Now, you feel a presence, a stillness, a peace. You no longer depend on the future for fulfillment and satisfaction — you don't look to it for salvation. Therefore, you are not attached to the results. Neither failure nor success has the power to change your inner state of Being. You have found the life underneath your life situation."

Stay true to yourself, do what you believe to be good work, and it will repay you.

CHAPTER 8: FINDING OUR IDENTITY

I often say something along the lines of, "We are what we do." When someone looks to define themselves, they simply need to look at what makes up their daily life.

Former Utah State University goalkeeper Jeannie Woller had the issue of defining herself once her soccer career ended.

In a Tedx Talk presented in 2016, Woller discussed the physical and mental toll she took after walking off the field for the final time.

Woller's problem? It wasn't losing soccer. It was the titles "soccer player" and "student-athlete." When she introduced herself, she could easily pull these titles out to define and represent who she was.

These titles were socially accepted and backed by an institution of higher learning. There was no confusion in who she was: a soccer player for USU. When someone else can backup that you are, in fact, represented by this title, there is no need to question it. That is an identity we can firmly stand behind.

For many people, falling into a socially-accepted identity is far easier than it seems. A high school student quickly becomes a college student who quickly finds a job. The transition from "student at University of Southern California" to "investment banker" is almost seamless. There is relatively no time to question who you are. Your title tells you.

"Even if we do decide to talk about [our identity, or lack thereof] on a larger platform like a Tedx stage and receive that validation, it is only internally that we can understand our true success," Woller said.

I faced a similar lack of identity once I graduated from college just as Woller did. While I didn't have athletic strings tying me to my school or feel like I was leaving any important part of my past behind by moving on to a life without school, it did feel odd to have finished my education.

It didn't feel weird at first. At my workplace, I was surrounded by peers that I enjoyed spending the summer with. Once the summer ended and they all went back to school, however, it finally hit me that for the first time in my life, I was not defined by a class schedule.

It becomes comforting to have that next year of school to look forward to, whether you like school or not. At least you know where you're going. The uneasiness of an undefined future rarely enters your mind. There are few questions to ponder about where you'll be in three, six, or twelve months while still in school.

Once my colleagues returned to school, my situation became apparent: I was an employee at a place I didn't even really like and nothing more.

The job search bearing no fruit only compounded my identity crisis: I'm a writer that no one will pay to write!

Even after starting my newsletter and journey on Medium, I still felt a lack of identity. I was writing, sure, but I didn't have that external institution confirming my status. How can I call myself a writer with no job?

It took me months to figure out what it took Woller months to figure out: our identity comes from within, not without. We are what we do—whether someone agrees with that or not.

One day, this reality hit me: I *am* a writer, so I should write. That same day, I began this book.

Now, if I'm ever confronted with the "Who are you?" question, my answer will be, "Writer," whether I have anything to show for it or not. I know that to be true within myself, whether an external figure agrees or not.

If Jeannie Woller and my examples don't relate to you, here is an article I recently wrote that goes a bit deeper.

How do you define yourself?

That is a question we should ask more often. Humans are both simple and complex. We are complex because we are constantly changing, whether on a grand or minute scale. Our beliefs evolve, our behaviors evolve, and our preferences and pleasures evolve.

We are simple because, for chunked periods of time, we are relatively consistent in what we do and what we like.

All of these likes, dislikes, behaviors, and actions define who we are. No one thing can completely display who we are — unless you are a celebrity, of course.

It is easy to weigh certain parts of our make-up more than others. If you are super passionate about running, you may tell others you're a runner. If you are a vegan and proud of it, you start to tell people. The more you act upon a behavior and discuss it with others, it starts to dominate your identity.

When acquaintances think of you, they may think "the runner" or "the vegan" and nothing more. Hell, you may even think that of yourself.

It is important to remember, though, that we do evolve and change over time — consciously and subconsciously. If you're "the runner" but eventually begin to hate running (or physically can't run anymore), what are you then? There are other things that go into your identity, but do you even know what they are?

This paragraph from James Clear's "Atomic Habits" discusses the idea of a diversified identity:

One solution is to avoid making any single aspect of your identity an overwhelming portion of who you are. In the words of investor Paul Graham, "keep your identity small." The more you let a single belief define you, the less capable you are of adapting when life challenges you. If you tie everything up in being the point guard or the partner at the firm or whatever else, then the loss of that facet of your life will wreck you.

I think everyone, in some way, is guilty of a narrow identity. When I think of myself, I think, "writer," as I discussed in the previous chapter. People in my life probably see me that way, too.

A way to get away from this narrow-minded view of ourselves is to break down what we do most into why we do what we do most. Some examples from "Atomic Habits":

"I'm an athlete" becomes *"I'm the type of person who is mentally tough and loves a physical challenge."*

"I'm a great soldier" transforms into *"I'm the type of person who is disciplined, reliable, and great on a team."*

"I'm the CEO" translates to *"I'm the type of person who builds and creates things."*

When you attempt to define yourself, look at what you do — whether it be your job, side-gig, or favorite hobby — and break down why you enjoy doing it.
I'll start. I'm not a writer; I'm a person that loves researching interesting topics, learning new things, and sharing my discoveries with the people of the world.

You could do this with the largest or smallest part of your identity. I'm not a sports fan; I'm loyal and stick through things whether it's easy or difficult. I see things through and am not afraid to critique the process if success is not being achieved.

Don't put yourself in a box. The pieces of you that help you achieve success and happiness in one area of life can be translated into other areas if you are willing to break your identity down into smaller pieces.

Start looking at what makes up your identity and asking more questions. That way, if that precious job, hobby, or accomplishment is stripped from you, you can take what you know and find something similar elsewhere.

There is another segment of an article I wrote just after deciding to break away from the girl I have discussed at length that is relevant here.

"Placing a piece of your identity onto the shoulders of another person will always cause heartache. People come and go, no matter what you tell yourself. In the search for a significant other, we often build a false reality in our heads. We think about the future and what could be. When it comes crashing down, it hurts. But not because something significant was taken away from us. The movie we directed in our head had a different ending than we originally planned."

CHAPTER 9: GIVING UP THE NEED FOR CONTROL

I think a significant portion of our suffering comes from our need to have control.

Wanting control over our lives is understandable. To some degree, we *do* need to control what is happening in our lives, otherwise it will start going in a direction we don't like. Our need to control everything, however, is limiting our ability to grow.

We are conditioned not to accept things because we are told to never stop chasing better. We are told to not accept a B in school —go for the A! We are taught to never settle for a partner below our standards.

These are things we *should* take control over. At some point in our development, though, the need to control seeps into areas where it shouldn't, causing us intense pain.

Perhaps the earliest lesson in rejection comes at the hands of that cute boy or girl in school. Before we caught feelings for a classmate, the only things we ever really wanted were toys or video games. Eventually you prioritize having a boyfriend or girlfriend over those material items and this is where pain enters the equation. Desire causes suffering, remember?

For some, rejection may come and go fairly easily. In this day and age, with Tinder and Instagram DMs popping off on a daily basis, the world of rejection is constantly at your fingertips. You don't even have to go outside to be called ugly anymore!

It seems easier for people these days to get rejected in real life, too, thanks to the internet. The younger generation has realized it can profit from getting rejected. Why not make a "Hitting on Girls!" video for YouTube or TikTok and see what happens? If you get rejected, it's good content, at least.

While these *do* count as rejections, they aren't actually real. Having some stranger tell you to leave them alone is not that big of a deal. Having someone closer to you do that, however, can create those wounds.

It's hard to simply tell someone to accept rejection and move on, because it's not that easy. As I discussed earlier, I faced rejection this year. And if you told me to just accept it while I was in my feelings about it, I would've been pissed off.

With rejection, the "four steps of grief" remedy seems to apply. Those four steps are: **shock/numbness, yearning/searching, disorganization/despair, reorganization/recovery.**

I don't believe it is possible for even the most enlightened person on earth to be able to skip any of these steps. But I do believe it is possible to shorten their duration.

While "shock" may not apply as much to losing a relationship rather than a loved one, "numbness" certainly can. Being told "thanks but no thanks" by a guy/girl you care about can leave you raw, emotionally scraping by for the following days, weeks, or months. I have never served in the military, but I would equate it to being hit by an emotional stun grenade: you're temporarily blinded and disoriented. Continuing to fight on doesn't feel worthwhile in the moment.

It's hard for me to give advice on speeding up the recovery of losing a long-term relationship filled with deep love and connection because I simply haven't had that experience. There is advice out there from experts that will surely help.

What I can advise on, however, is something we discussed earlier: identity. A relationship of any kind can become part of our identity. When you are deeply fond of someone, you don't want to lose them. They may be a part of your everyday life and removing them would almost feel like you're not *you* anymore.

This is where it is important to remember that anything external can be removed. Anything given can be taken. Attaching yourself to a person may cause incredible happiness now, but it could cause tremendous pain later on.

Like everything else, there is a balance to relationships. For the good days there are the bad, for the happy moments there are the sad, and for the connections there are the departures.

I am not advising you to pull away from your partner so you don't get hurt later on. I am saying that it is important to remind yourself that you are complete no matter what you find in this material world. Making this person your "world" is not healthy. What's left when they leave?

You are left. You are the only thing you'll ever have that cannot leave. Constantly remind yourself of that, if necessary.

The "yearning/searching" phase can hang around for a while. It's weird to go from talking to/seeing someone on a daily basis and all of a sudden losing that presence indefinitely/permanently.

This was a difficult phase for me in my most recent "love interest." Filling a hole the size of an entire person is not easy. When you care for them and talk with them throughout the day, it's odd to not have it anymore. It gives you a sense of emptiness.

You may challenge yourself with the "What could have been?" questions or "What do I do now?" It's probably a mix of both. Figuring out where to go next is the tough part, however, because you don't want to move forward without that person beside you.

The great discovery of this phase is realizing that, now, you are in control. This mixes into the next phase: disorganization/despair.

Your life feels like a mess. The effects of that love stun grenade still reside. Life is blurry and your head hurts. Why even get out of bed?

I went back to my back patio, taking in nature and staring at the blue sky. I felt the need to get away. I poked at the idea of joining the Peace Corps or finding some other way to dedicate my time to helping the less fortunate. I felt like a rapid change was needed in my life to recover and feel whole again.

Eventually, you get over it and realize things will be OK. Your life moves on and you find things to fill that hole. Maybe you even realize there never really was a hole.

Now, you're in "reorganization/recovery." How did you get here? Well, you went through a lot of emotions, thought a lot, let time do it's thing. But most importantly, you accepted the situation. You gave up control of the situation and let destiny—if you believe in that kind of thing—do it's dance.

The earlier you realize how little you have control over where you end up and who you end up with, the better prepared you are for a future of rejection and loss.

I don't want to tell you that you have *no* control of your life, because that's simply not true (in my opinion, at least). You could go really deep and question if free will is actually instilled in us, but that's a discussion for someone else to start.

You have an immense amount of control in creating situations and opportunities for yourself, but you have little control on the outcomes of those situations/opportunities.

If you want to make more friends or get a girlfriend/boyfriend, put on your best face and go socialize. Join a club or a class and start talking to people. Will they like you? You don't know that. But you can control putting yourself out there, so do that and see what happens.

If you want a better job, learn more skills. Add those skills to your resume and apply for better jobs. Will they hire you? You don't know that. But you can control beefing up your resume, so do that and see what happens.

Focusing on the process rather than the results is the most reliable and trustworthy method of attaining both more material success and more peace of mind. Focusing on outcomes (money, views, sales, etc.) will leave you frustrated because those outcomes rely on other people. Those people will not always come through. You may get mad at them, which brings more negativity into your mind. Or you may get mad at yourself, which only sets you back in moving forward.

Focusing on the process will invoke an emotional response based on what *you* put in. You have all the control over this. If you are a musician that puts out an album that you love, you should be proud of that, even if it only sells 10 copies. You have to believe that the universe will reward your effort and love for the process by delivering you success, even if it means producing 10 great albums beforehand.

This is why one of my main goals in life is to not spend all my years working for another person. Much of today's work is built around impressing at least one boss and his/her goals. Oftentimes it is more than one boss, such as companies with a large corporate structure.

For me personally, I can only care so much about a job if the things out of my control aren't handled properly. If there are mistakes happening because of a co-worker's lack of care or in other parts of the company, I am not going to constantly go out my way to fix these mistakes. I control what is in front of me and spend little time worrying about covering up for other people's errors.

I have become this way because of past experiences of constantly trying to fix people's mistakes. Or, at the very least, getting upset because these mistakes were being made.

My current employer has been trying to give me a promotion for months. A past version of myself would have taken this promotion. Making more money is awesome! There is always a tradeoff to making more money, however. And if you recall much of the book leading up to this point, you'll know that money isn't enough to entice me.

My main reasoning behind rejecting this offer was because of how much would be out of my control. The job is essentially managing other people's mistakes and being a daily problem solver. I don't mind waking up everyday and fixing other people's problems. But I'd rather do it through a venture such as this one than to help some rich folks get richer.

Becoming accepting of the moment and managing what you can control can be applied to almost any facet of your life. That girl doesn't like you? It's OK, there will be another one. That job didn't hire you? That's too bad, but another one will want you soon. Your friend is being annoying? Talk to them about it or maybe give yourself some space.

Your need to control your entire life and its outcomes will drag you down into a deep, dark hole. Realize your wholeness, focus on the process, accept things out of your control, and you will see brighter days and more material success in response.

CONCLUSION

Writing this book was an interesting way to reflect on the year 2020—one of which many will remember as terribly awful. The year people lost their job, the year people lost their loved ones, the year people lost their ability to carelessly live their lives without having to worry about getting sick.

For some, like me, it was the year we lost ourselves. It was the year we faced adversity like never before and were able to make it through to the other side with some gained perspective.

For me, it was a year of lessons—lessons that you have now read. And if this book did its job, it helped prevent you from making mistakes, or will help you from making them in the future. It helped you get over that crush, it helped you cut out the non-essential bullcrap. It helped you find your purpose and it helped you discover your true inner self.

Maybe it helped you realize that your story and path is your own and comparison will leave you getting in your own way. Maybe it helped you define your identity and let go of the things that are out of your control.

At the very least, I hope it made you think (while at the same time made you *stop* thinking). I hope you took these lessons, many of which go against the grain of traditional societal standards and practices, seriously. I hope you gave the content real thought and tried applying the lessons to where you currently are in life.

While this book is intended for people like me—fresh-out-of-college young adults that don't quite know what the hell is going on yet—I think a person of any age could appreciate, or perhaps even learn from, the lessons I learned and the words I wrote. People can learn these lessons at any time—there is no specific age at which they could come into someone's life.

If you loved or hated the words, disagreed with something said, have a story to share, or questions to ask, please reach out to me on Twitter @ByDylanHughes or email me at **writtenbydylan@gmail.com**. Let's learn from each other and help make the world a better place, one small step at a time.

Printed in Great Britain
by Amazon